Witzy loves the water.

Hello, Peek-a-boo!

Spring showers will bring flowers.

Witzy can make his name with his blocks.

Lulla loves to smell flowers.
How many flowers do you see in this picture?

Your answer:

Answer: 5

Everyone has a lucky star!

Which picture is different?

A

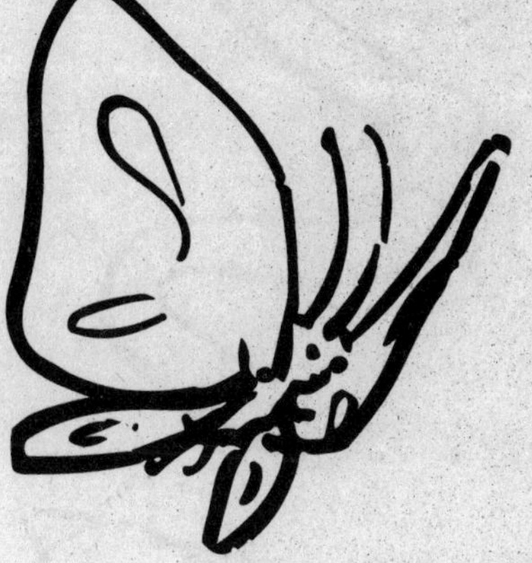

B

C

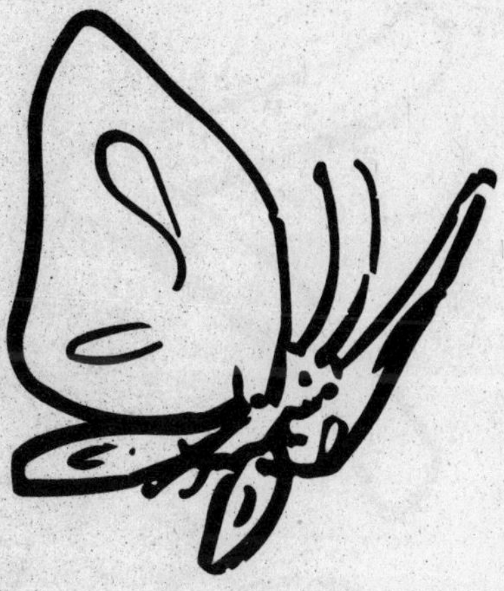

D

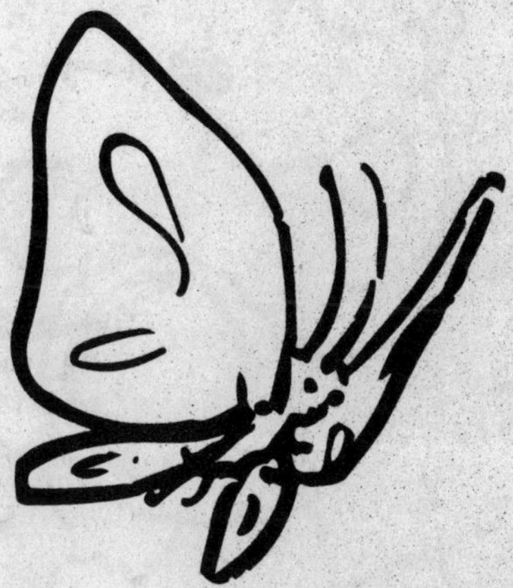

E

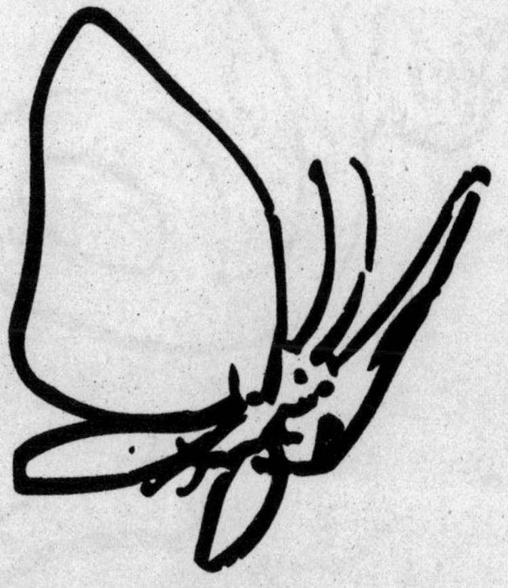

Your answer:

Answer: E

Help Boof count his numbers
by coloring them in.

Let's go for a ride, Lulla!

Shh... Boof is napping.

Lulla is hanging out with everybody.
How many birds can you count in the picture?

Your answer: ◯

Answer: 4

Lulla is a musical bunny.

Witzy is making a sound like a train.
Can you draw a picture of a train?

Give me a W!

Make words using the letters in:

BIRTHDAY PARTY

Where are you off to, Tickle bugs?

Use the grid to draw Lulla.

A nosy Tickle bug!

Lulla hears something.
Draw what you think it is.

Tickle bugs love to perch on Witzy's bill.

Help Boof, Lulla, and Patches find Witzy.

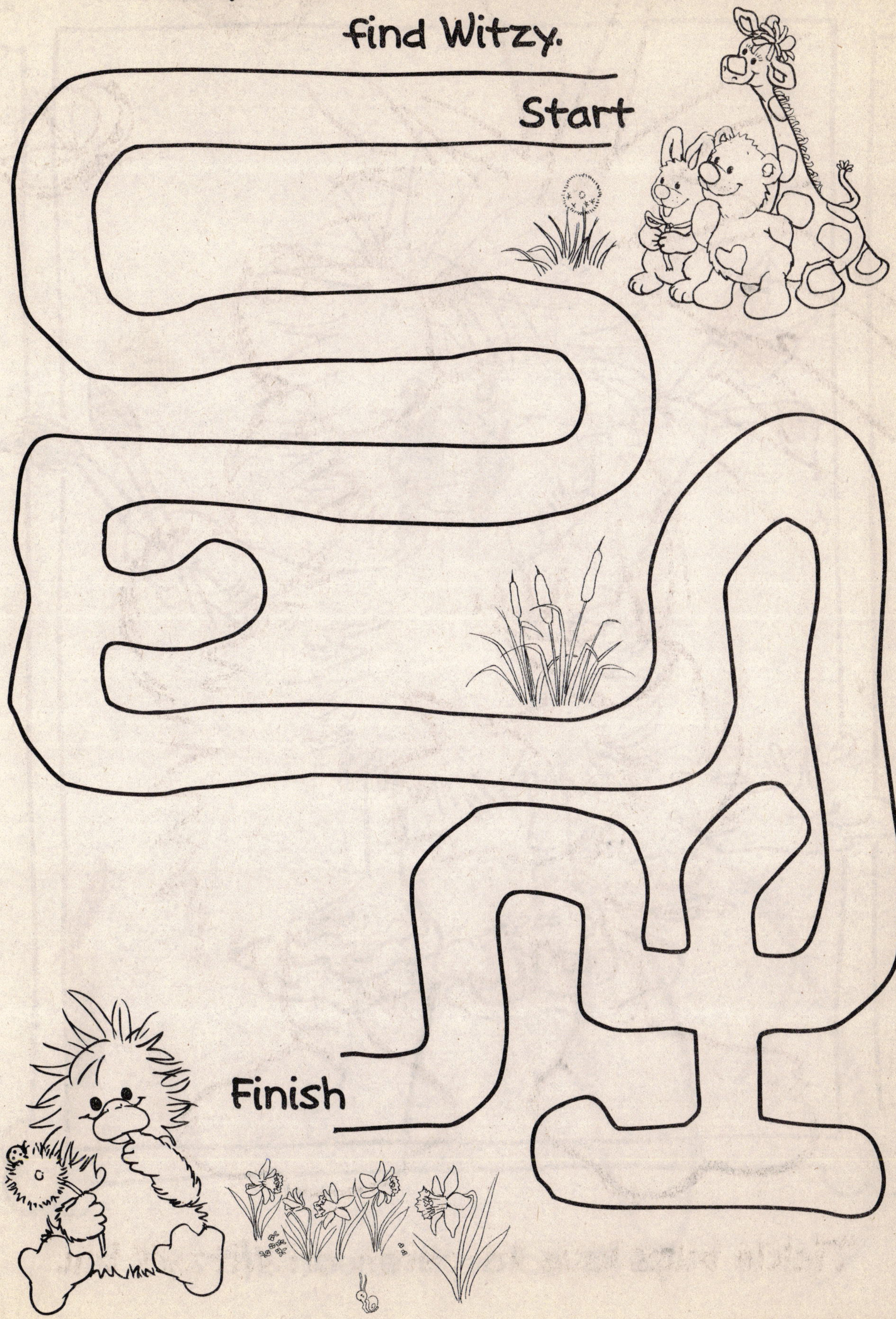

Let's color the world!

"Oof!" says Boof.

Sweet friends!

Snacking is thirsty work.

Draw a picture of Flootie the butterfly!

Peek-a-boo is a careful painter.

Let's go, team!

Match the drawings on the left with the ones on the right.

How many balls do you count?
Color them in.

Your answer: ◯

Answer: 7

Witzy and his friends sail away
on a giant lily pad!

Patches waters the garden.

What a fun party!

What is Zoom Zoom telling Lulla?
Write or draw it inside the frame.

Peek-a-boo wants to share a strawberry.

Where is Dragon?

How many Tickle bugs does Witzy count?
Color them in.

Your answer: ◯

Answer: 8

Stomp, stomp go Patches' galoshes.

Lulla loves to brush her soft fur every day.

Lulla and Peek-a-boo dance to a lively tune.

How many birds does Boof see?

Your answer: ◯

Answer: 12

Lulla and Patches love to dance together.

Songs for a princess.

Which picture is different?

A

B

C

D

Your answer:

Answer: D

Patches is so tall!

The frogs get ready to sing.

Lulla has a hop-hop-happy day.

Mmm! Lulla loves to smell nice!

Witzy loves his rubber ducky.

Help Witzy pass the ball to Lulla by completing the maze.

Boof soars through the sky!

Lulla and Patches are going for a ride. Can you write words that describe where they're going?

Will you come to my party, Lulla?

Sunshine makes Lulla smile.

Witzy says, "Catch me!"

Lulla loves butterflies!

Help Boof count the blocks
and color them in.

Love makes you light-hearted!

Make words using the letters in:

FOOTBALL

What a breezy pleasy day!

Which picture is different?

A

B

C

D

Your answer:

Answer: B

Go for the touchdown, Boof!

Good catch, Lulla!

Which picture is different?

Your answer:

Answer: B